# VALENTINE
## CRAFTS and COOKBOOK

M. GROSSMAN

# VALENTINE
## CRAFTS and COOKBOOK

BY GARDNER QUINN

With Illustrations by Madeline Grossman

**HARVEY HOUSE**

Library of Congress Catalog Card Number 77-78093
Manufactured in the United States of America
ISBN 0-8178-5592-0

Harvey House, Publishers
20 Waterside Plaza, New York, New York 10010

Published in Canada by Fitzhenry & Whiteside Ltd., Toronto

## For Your Valentine

*Roses are red,*
*Violets are blue,*
*This Valentine book*
*Is just for you!*

Valentine's Day is a perfect holiday for doing something special for your family and friends. All of your favorite people like being remembered on February 14. The presents and messages they like best are the ones you make yourself because they show how much you really care.

This little book is filled with Valentine's Day gift and menu ideas that are beautiful, easy and fun to make. If you want February 14 to be a very special day, this is just the book for you.

Valentine's Day means bright red and pink hearts, flowers, candy and special messages to people we love. Some Valentine messages are sweet and sentimental, some are funny, and some express friendship. The custom of *sending* these messages started more than fifteen hundred years ago!

In the year 270 A.D., the Roman emperor Claudius wanted all male citizens of his empire to be free of family ties so that they could march with his armies. To make sure they would be free, Claudius did an unbelievable thing— he outlawed marriage!

A priest named Valentine disobeyed the emperor by performing secret wedding ceremonies for couples in love. Valentine was caught and put in prison, and the emperor soon ordered his execution. On February 14, the day he was to die, Valentine sent a grateful message to the jailer's young daughter (she had been kind to him during his imprisonment). This is how the custom of sending thoughtful messages on Valentine's Day began. Valentine, the sympathetic priest who died because he believed in love, is now remembered as Saint Valentine, the patron saint of lovers.

Since that first Valentine's Day greeting was sent hundreds of years ago, other ways to celebrate February 14 have come to be. Giving special gifts, writing poems, making sweet desserts and having colorful parties are some of them. Each says "I care" to people you really love.

# Making Valentines

Making your own cards and writing your own special messages are good ways to celebrate Valentine's Day. You can draw or make hearts, flowers, Cupid and his bow and arrow, and birds (especially doves) for your special greetings. Cards can be made in any shape or size from a variety of materials.

These are some things you can use:

> Paper: construction (red and pink are especially nice), metallic, tissue, crepe, cellophane and plain white
>
> Lace paper doilies (some stores sell heart-shaped ones)
>
> Paste
>
> Scissors
>
> Crayons, ball point or felt pens of different colors

You can also use: cloth scraps, buttons, candy hearts, cutouts from magazines or old greeting cards, ribbons, lace, needle and thread, pieces of cardboard, felt scraps, yarn.

The lace doilies can be cut into flower, star, or snowflake shapes. You can make flowers and hearts from tissue and crepe paper. You can make pictures with cloth or by using your crayons and pens. You can edge your cards with lace or frame them with lace paper doilies. Use your imagination to create cards for special people, and write a thoughtful poem or message inside each one.

Would Mother like a large lacy heart?

Would your brother like a funny message tucked under his door?

Grandmother will like *any* card you make.

Some simple messages for your handmade cards are:

*Be my Valentine*
*My heart is yours*

*I love you, Valentine*
*Please be mine*

About a hundred years ago, during the Victorian Age, people sent elaborate cards that cost as much as ten dollars each. Some cards cost even more. The messages on these very fancy cards were often sentimental and poetic:

*Remember me,*
*As I will thee.*

Like a peaceful, gliding river
May thy life forever be.
And may the Giver of all good
Ever gently deal with thee.

May the hand of time
Never blot out these little words:
"Forget me not."

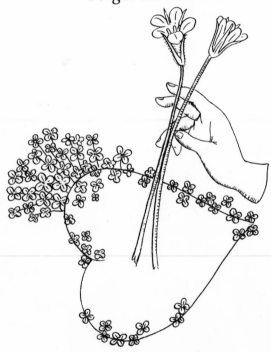

Plant a forget-me-not
In the garden of your heart
For me.

The roses of the valley may wither,
The flowers of the forest decay,
But our friendship shall last forever
Though all things fade away.

Remember me, and bear in mind
A truthful friend is hard to find.
And when you get one good and true,
Don't change an old one for a new.

The most famous verse of all is
*Roses are red,*
*Violets are blue,*
*Sugar is sweet,*
*And so are you.*

*Roses are red, violets are blue*
*Happy Valentine's Day from your friend—guess who!*

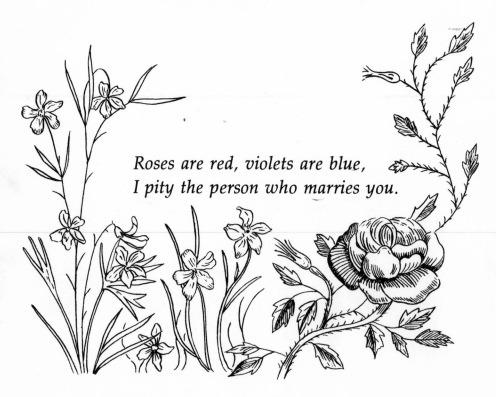

*Roses are red, violets are blue,*
*I pity the person who marries you.*

You can change this poem to make it funny, silly, or personal:

*Roses are red, violets are blue*
*You look like a monkey, who lives in a zoo.*

Most fun of all, of course, is to create your own message.

Flowers and candy are traditional Valentine's Day gifts. In fact, flowers have a language and meaning all their own which you might want to learn. For example, red roses mean "I love you," yellow roses mean "I am jealous," white roses mean "I am worthy of you," and four-leaf clovers mean "be mine." Garden flowers are not in bloom in many parts of the country during February. So, if you'd like to give flowers as gifts on Valentine's Day, think about *making* them.

Look around the house and see if you can find some pieces of colored cloth. (Cotton is especially good because it starches well.)

You will need some thin wire for connecting your cloth petals and some heavier wire for making stems. If you have ever worked with 'flower-maker' kits, or if someone in your house likes to arrange flowers, you probably have these wires on hand. If not, your florist can supply them at little cost.

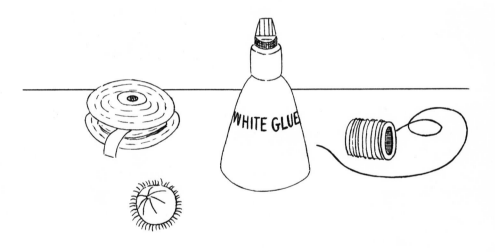

You will also need some green florist's tape, some ball fringe, and white glue (the kind that comes in plastic bottles).

17

Here is what you do:
Cut your fabric in pieces large enough so you can cut five petals for each flower in shapes like this later on. Then mix up a solution of one part glue to three parts water and soak your pieces of fabric in it.

Hang these pieces up to dry and then cut them into petals. You do not have to iron the fabric.

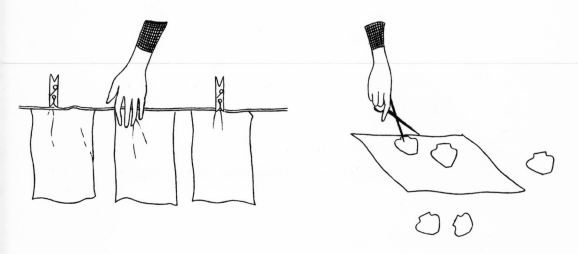

Now attach a ball from your fringe to a stem wire with some florist's tape. This will be the center of the flower.

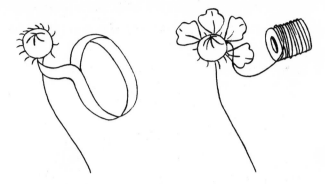

Add your petals one by one by attaching them to the stem wire with the thin wire.

When you have the petals in place, cover the stem wire with the green tape.

After you have practiced making the petals, you can vary their shapes.

## Paper Flowers

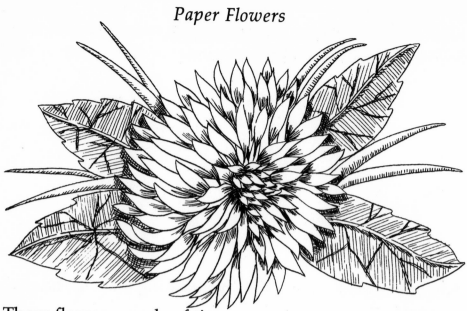

These flowers, made of tissue paper, are pretty and fun to make.

Some things you will need:

A compass with a pencil that has thick, dark lead

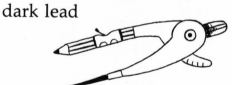

Tissue wrapping paper in Valentine's Day colors

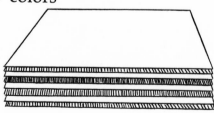

 Scissors

Thin florist's wire like the kind you used for the fabric flowers

Stem wires

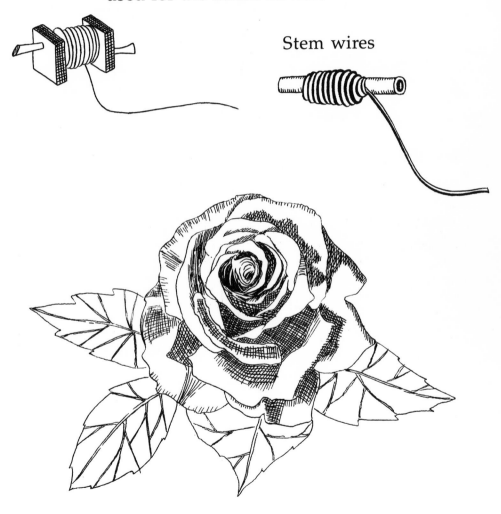

Take your compass and draw at least 10 circles of equal size (small, medium or big) on a sheet of newspaper. Then take a sheet of tissue wrapping paper and place it on top of the newspaper. Your heavy circles will show right through, so you'll be able to trace them onto the tissue.

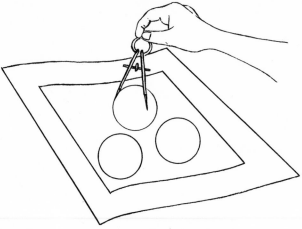

When you're done tracing, take your scissors and cut out ten circles from your tissue paper.

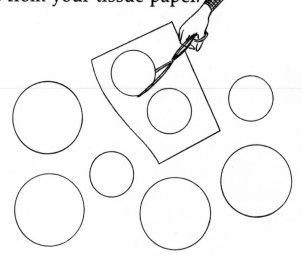

Now fold one circle at a time into a fan fold. Do not unfold. Take your thin wire and wrap it around one folded circle at a time (one on top of another).

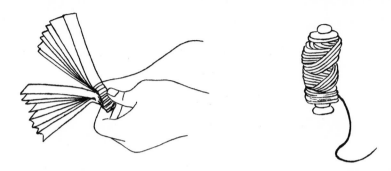

When you have wrapped all ten folded circles, spread out the tissue circles and fluff and shape them. Then attach them to a stem wire.

After you have practiced shaping petals you can get some wonderful variations by cutting your circles big for the bottom petals, medium-sized for the middle petals and smaller for the top petals so you can get a peony or layered effect. You can cut out as many petals for each flower as you like.

## Forget-Me-Not Candy

What could be more in keeping with Valentine's Day than pink and white candy that you have made yourself? It's easy to do, and does not need cooking. Here are the ingredients:

> 1 egg white
> 2 cups sifted confectioners' sugar
> 2 teaspoons butter
> ½ teaspoon vanilla
> redhots and silver shot

Put all the ingredients into a mixing bowl and stir until creamy. Separate half the mixture and put it into another bowl. Tint one batch pink with a small amount of red food coloring.

Drop small spoonfuls onto waxed paper and decorate with heart-shaped red hots or silver shot. Let stand to become firm.

### Lovable Lollipops

One of your favorite people would love some homemade lollipops all arranged in a pretty candy box. This is an easy recipe but be sure you have three things—a candy thermometer, an adult to be with you because the cooking mixture is hot, and some thin candy sticks (don't get the flat ones that look like tongue depressors because they don't work very well).

Here is the recipe:

> 2 cups sugar
> ½ cup light corn syrup
> Flavoring extract (vanilla is probably
>    the most popular)
> Red food coloring

In a heavy saucepan combine the sugar, corn syrup and a half cup of water.

Put your candy thermometer in the pan and cook the mixture without stirring it until the thermometer reads 300 degrees.

Now add your flavoring and coloring and stir the ingredients just enough to mix them.

Lay out your wooden sticks about 2 inches apart on a buttered cookie sheet (or aluminum foil if you'd rather). Pour some of the candy mixture over the tops of each stick.

When the lollipops have cooled, wrap each one in waxed paper or cellophane and arrange them in your candy box. You'll have about a pound of candy.

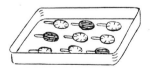

## Decorated Valentine Boxes

Cover an empty oatmeal box or a square tea box with red paper or red cellophane. You can glue it on with rubber cement or you can buy adhesive-backed paper.

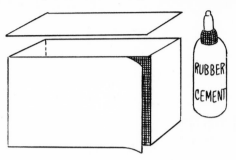

Decorate with flowers cut out of paper or cloth and with tiny ribbon bows. Add a rim of lace edging or ribbon at the top, just below the rim. Decorate the lid in the same way. Fill the box with your favorite sweets or Valentine cookies that you've made yourself (see page 32).

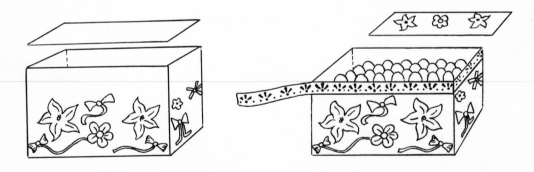

(You can decorate a small square box this same way and use it as a jewelry box. Line the inside with felt.)

### Stone Paperweight

Find a large, smooth stone about the size of your fist. Scrub it well and let it dry thoroughly—probably overnight. You can also let it dry on a radiator or in the hot sun.

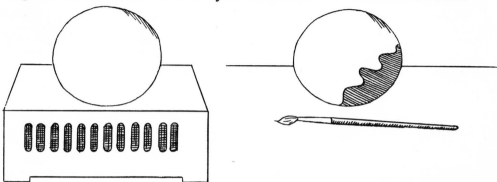

Spread newspapers over the area you will be working in. Now you can paint the stone all one color with tempera or enamel paint. Wait until the stone is dry. Then paint birds or hearts and flowers on it in contrasting colors. You can shellac your stone after the paint is totally dry. A white background with pink and red decoration is a good color combination for a Valentine's Day paperweight!

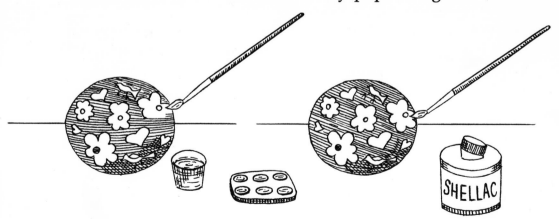

## A Party

Why not give a party on St. Valentine's Day!? You can decorate your table with a Valentine tree. Find some fallen, dry tree branches about two or three feet long and place them in a container filled with modelling clay (a container of pebbles or sand is also good). Spray-paint the branches white. Then, using thread, hang hearts of all shapes and sizes cut out from felt and paper onto the branches. Cut out some birds and flowers, too. This makes a pretty centerpiece on a red tablecloth. You can use white lace doilies as placemats for an added touch.

### RED AND WHITE SANDWICHES

Cut slices of bread with a heart-shaped cookie cutter.
Spread each one with softened cream cheese. Then top
each sandwich with a small mound of red jelly or jam—
raspberry, strawberry, or red currant.

### STRAWBERRY OR RASPBERRY MILK

For each serving, mix (or blend in the blender) one cup of
milk and two heaping teaspoons of jam, topping, or ber-
ries. Add 2 or 3 drops of red coloring, if desired.

## SUGAR COOKIES

| | |
|---|---|
| 2 cups sifted flour | 1 cup sugar |
| 1½ teaspoons baking powder | |
| 1 egg | ½ teaspoon salt |
| 1 teaspoon vanilla | |
| ½ cup shortening | 1 tablespoon cream or whole milk |

(If you want to make *Spice* Sugar Cookies, leave *out* the vanilla and add ¼ teaspoon each of cinnamon, allspice, and cloves to the flour.)

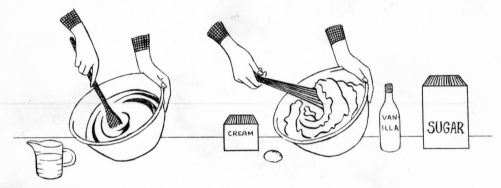

Mix and sift 1½ cups of flour. Add the baking powder and salt.

In a large bowl, cream the shortening until it is soft. Then beat in the sugar, the egg, the cream and the vanilla. Stir the sifted flour into this mixture, and gradually add the remaining ½ cup of flour until the dough is just stiff enough to roll flat.

Chill the dough about 25 minutes. Then place it on a lightly-floured pastry board and roll it to a ⅛" thickness. Take your heart-shaped and flower-shaped cookie cutters and dust them with some flour. Then cut out your cookies and place them on an ungreased cookie sheet. Sprinkle with a little extra sugar and bake them for 8-10 minutes in a 375-400° oven. You can decorate them with red sugar sprinkles or cinnamon hearts while they're cooling. (Store them *after* they cool in a tightly covered tin or jar!)
Yield: 4 to 5 dozen cookies.

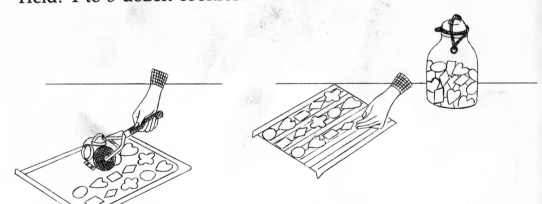

## SWEETHEART DESSERT

Here is a Sweetheart Dessert that is delicious and very easy to make:

In a medium-sized mixing bowl, dissolve 1 package of raspberry gelatin in 1 cup of boiling water. While this mixture is still hot add 1 small package of frozen raspberries, breaking them up gently. By now the mixture is only slightly warm, or even cool. Take a mixing spoon and dip

6 or so rather large spoonfuls of vanilla ice cream into your mixture. Swirl the ice cream around like you do when you make marble cake. Put the bowl of dessert in the freezer. It will be ready in a half hour. Scoop it into tall glasses and serve it with some cookies. Your guests will say you're a 'sweetheart.'

## Valentine Cupcakes

Valentine cupcakes should be easy for you to make because you can use a prepared cake mix and let your imagination do the rest. Look in your supermarket for a cake mix that has a pink tint. If you can't find one, you can tint a white cake mix pink with food coloring. You can also use a white cake mix and color your frosting pink or red. Follow the directions on the box for making your cupcakes.

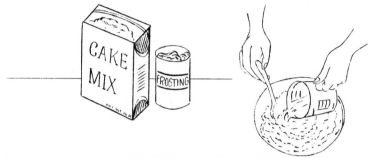

Using paper or foil liners in your cupcake or muffin pans is much neater than coating them with butter. When your cupcakes are cool, you can frost them with a package icing. If your icing is pink, you can form it into a heart design on each cupcake. If your icing is white, you can sprinkle it with some pink-tinted coconut.

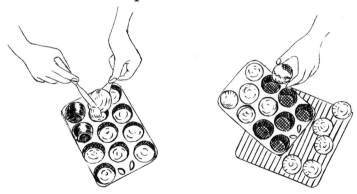

## HEART-SHAPED COCONUT CAKE

If Mother has two 8" or 9" heart-shaped cake pans, maybe you would rather make a cake for Valentine's Day. Use a white packaged cake, mix, and divide your batter evenly between the two pans. When the cakes are cool,

spread some red jam or jelly on one layer and put the other layer neatly on top of it. Make some white frosting from a package and after you spread that on, decorate the sides (or the whole cake) with coconut. This will look very pretty on your Valentine table.

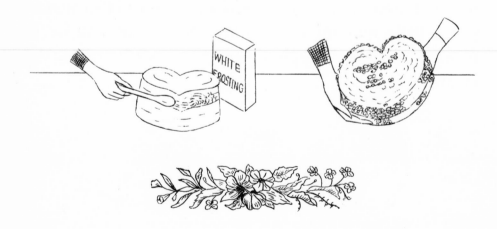

## HEARTS-AND-FLOWERS SALAD

If Mother has heart-shaped cake pans, she is probably the kind of organized person who also has small heart-shaped salad molds. In that case, you can make a *Hearts-and-Flowers Salad*. Use a red gelatin mix, and, after you have stirred it up, let it thicken slightly in your refrigerator. Open a small can of fruit salad, separate the fruit from the liquid, and add the fruit to your mixture.

Now divide the gelatin into the individual molds. Let them set in the refrigerator. When you're ready to serve, unmold them onto dishes lined with pieces of lettuce and put a little mayonnaise on top. Your fruit will be the flowers peeking through the molded heart. That was very creative!

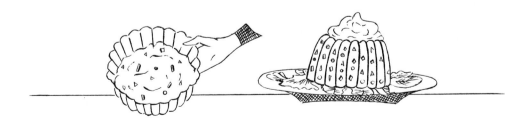

## RED-HOT APPLE SAUCE

Why not whip up a batch of apple sauce and put in some cinnamon candy hearts while the sauce is still warm? The hearts will melt and color the mixture red-pink and give it a terrific flavor. Here is the basic recipe for apple sauce.

Carefully take the skin off and remove the core from 8 cooking apples. (Your mother can tell you what kind of apples to use for cooking and show you the right way to peel and core them.) After this is done you can cut your apples into smaller pieces and put them in a pan with about 1" of water. Cover the pan and let the apples cook

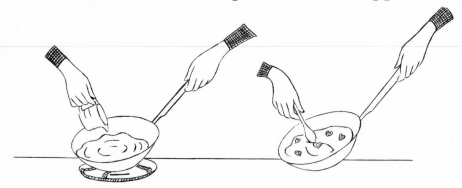

under low heat (simmer) for 15 or 20 minutes. Then add a half cup of sugar and bring the mixture to a boil. Now is the time to remove the pan from the heat and stir in your red-hots. You are one good cook!

## PINK PARFAIT

By now you've probably done so much work that you'd like a nice simple recipe. You're in luck if Mother has some parfait or sherbet glasses.

All you need to do is put small layers of strawberry ice cream and whipped cream or dessert topping in the glass. Build up the alternating layers and finish with a nice big splash of the topping decorated with red sprinkles. This dessert is best made when you're ready to serve it because putting the glasses in the freezer makes the mixture too hard.

*Match Your Food to the Days*

The best kind of party planning and food preparation is the kind that you create yourself by matching up (coordinating) your menu and decorations with the holiday or special event being celebrated. St. Valentine's Day is an easy holiday to plan for because the colors are red and pink and white and the symbols are hearts, flowers and other gentle things. Make a list for yourself of all the foods and trimmings that suit this holiday. Here are a few menu items to start your list. How many more can you think of?

Jellied cranberry sauce (from a can) cut in heart shapes with a cookie cutter

Shiny, crispy red apples

Pink and white mint wafers

Radish flowers

Artichoke hearts (No? Well, some people like them!)

Vanilla pudding with candy hearts on top

Heart-shaped French toast (cut bread with cookie cutter)

Apple rings

Sour cream and onion dip decorated with pimento cherries and cherry tomatoes (We're rushing the holidays a little, but Washington's Birthday is coming right up!)

## The Hit of the Party

Do you have a little brother or a little boy who is your friend? Does he have a toy bow-and-arrow set? Will he let you attach wings to his back? If so, you can have him arrive at your party dressed as Cupid, the Roman god of love. You'd better show him a picture of Cupid when you ask him to play this part. He won't do it? Well, your party has been put together so lovingly that it will be a success anyway!

## Some Valentine Superstitions and Customs

If you are a girl, the first boy you see on Valentine's Day is destined to become your husband. If you are a boy, the first girl you see on February 14th will become your wife.

Legends tell us that birds choose their mates on February 14, and that whatever bird you first see on that day tells your future:

If a girl sees a robin, she will marry a sailor.

If she sees a sparrow, she will marry a poor man, but she will be happy.

Spotting a goldfinch means she will marry a millionaire.

A flock of doves indicates good fortune in a marriage. Seeing a white dove fly overhead is a sign of good luck, and dreaming about a dove is said to be a promise of happiness.

According to legend, people fall in love because Cupid, the little god of love, pierces their hearts with his arrow.

For hundreds of years young men gave their sweethearts a pair of gloves on Valentine's Day. The gloves symbolized asking for a young woman's "hand" in marriage.

In early times, people took Valentine's Day very seriously and considered it a very important holiday. Today, *we* think of it as a special time to show love and appreciation of those we care about—just as St. Valentine did long, long ago. If you celebrate this day with the right spirit, you will enjoy it very much.

And remember: while you've been working so hard making such marvelous things for your family and friends, they have probably been busy creating thoughtful surprises for you! That's what Valentine's Day is all about!

*Roses are Red*
*Violets are blue*
*We hope that these pages*
*were helpful to you!*
HAPPY VALENTINE'S DAY!

Madeline Grossman graduated from the Maryland Institute College of Art with a BFA in art education, and a minor in book illustration. A resident of New York City, she works as a free-lance artist bringing experience as a designer, colorist, calligrapher, and illustrator to her work. Ms. Grossman's drawings for VALENTINE CRAFTS AND COOKBOOK are rich in the sentiment found in Victorian Valentines.